Sometimes when I consider what

tremendous consequences come

from little things, I am tempted

to think there are no little things.

BRUCE BARTON

the little things

Compiled by Kobi Yamada
Designed by Steve Potter and Jenica Wilkie

COMPENDIUM
PUBLISHING

live inspired.

This book is dedicated to all of you who make a big difference.

Acknowledgements

These quotations were gathered lovingly but unscientifically over several years and/or contributed by many friends or acquaintances. Some arrived—and survived in our files— on scraps of paper and may therefore be imperfectly worded or attributed. To the authors, contributors and original sources, our thanks, and where appropriate, our apologies.
—*The editors*

With special thanks to

Jason Aldrich, Gerry Baird, Jay Baird, Neil Beaton, Doug Cruickshank, Jim Darragh, Kari & Kyle Diercks, Josie & Rob Estes, Jennifer Hurwitz, Liam Lavery, Connie McMartin, Cristal & Brad Olberg, Janet Potter & Family, Aimee Rawlins, Diane Roger, Sam Sundquist, Drew Wilkie, Robert & Mary Anne Wilkie, Heidi & Shale Yamada, Justi, Tote & Caden Yamada, Robert & Val Yamada, Kaz & Kristin Yamada, Tai & Joy Yamada, Anne Zadra, August & Arline Zadra, Gus & Rosie Zadra and Dan Zadra.

Credits

Compiled by Kobi Yamada
Designed by Steve Potter & Jenica Wilkie

ISBN: 1-932319-17-4

Printed in China

The little things in life? The little moments? They aren't little. They often turn out to be the most memorable and meaningful things we encounter. We may not recognize them while they are happening, or have the words to describe how they make us feel. We may seldom talk about them, but they affect us deeply.

If we sat down to think about the precious little things in life—those that make our lives more vibrant, connected and inspired—we would find genuine, heartfelt moments that shape our lives and make us who we are. Little things like a job well done, someone being there for you, an honest compliment, taking time to play, and being a good person. The little things really are the cornerstone of a full life.

We can't take the little things for granted. They have built companies, friendships and just about everything of value. No act of generosity, kindness or service is ever wasted, no matter how small. Everything matters. Everything we do helps or hurts, adds up or takes away. We need to count on each other for the little things that make life so big. In the end, it is not the days or the years that we remember, but the moments.

A purposeful life.

We all need something to believe in, something for which we can have whole-hearted enthusiasm. We need to feel that our life has meaning, that we are needed in this world.

HANNAH SENESH

The future is not someplace we are going to, but a place we are creating. The paths to it are not found, they are made. JANE GARVEY

An exciting vision.

Dreams pass into the reality of action.

From the actions stems the dream again;

and this interdependence produces the

highest form of living. ANAIS NIN

Following your dreams.

Making it happen.

Today is the day.

UNKNOWN

Trying something new.

Unless you walk out into the unknown, the odds of making a profound difference in your life are pretty low. TOM PETERS

By being yourself, you put something

wonderful in the world that was

not there before. EDWIN ELLIOT

Embracing your uniqueness.

It seems to me that we can never give up longing or wishing while we are alive. There are certain things we feel to be beautiful and good, and we must hunger for them. GEORGE ELIOT

Finding the good.

Listening to your heart.

Follow your passion as long as you live. PTAH-HOTEP

Creating positive change.

Person to person,

moment to moment,

as we love, we change

the world. SAMAHRIA KAUFMAN

From small beginnings come great things.

PROVERB

Getting started.

Living
with
intention.

We each have only a limited amount of time here.

We have to do more with it, pay attention, explore, be open

to all of life. Because we have only one chance, we have to

make life seem longer than it really is. VIGGO MORTENSEN

May you always find new roads

to travel; new horizons to explore;

new dreams to call your own. UNKNOWN

A daring adventure.

Doing what you love.

Finding the right work is

like discovering your soul

in the world. THOMAS MOORE

Loving what you do.

What we love and what captures our curiosity draws us forward into some place of great destiny. WAYNE MULLER

Finding
success.

You've achieved
success in your field
when you don't know
whether what you're
doing is work or play.

WARREN BEATTY

No matter what your role

is in the business of life,

the goal is quality and the

challenge is reaching it.

FRED SMITH

Creating value.

A job well-done.

Whoever I am or whatever I am doing, some kind of excellence is within my reach.

JOHN GARDNER

Be fanatics. When it comes to being, doing and dreaming the best, be maniacs. A.M. ROSENTHAL

Exceeding expectations.

Keeping your word.

Live and work with integrity, and everything else is a piece of cake.

PAT SALVATORE

Finding

Everything is always impossible before it works. HUNT GREENE

a way.

Possibilities do not add up. They multiply. PAUL M. ROMER

Beating the odds.

Doing what you love.

Finding the right work is

like discovering your soul

in the world. THOMAS MOORE

Learning from mistakes.

Wrong turns

are as important

as right turns.

More important

sometimes.

RICHARD BACH

We are the hurdles we leap to be ourselves.   MICHAEL McCLURE

Overcoming obstacles.

There's a good time coming.

SIR WALTER SCOTT

Staying optimistic.

Taking
chances.

Go and wake up your luck. PERSIAN PROVERB

There's nothing
like the feeling
of sheer joy of
wanting to get
up and help the
world go around.

HEIDI WILLS

Something to hope for.

Having faith.

We must walk consciously only part way toward our goal, and then leap in the dark to our success.

HENRY DAVID THOREAU

Facing your fears.

Courage is adversity's lamp. VAUVENARGUES

You have a gift that only you can give

the world—that's the whole reason you're

on the planet. Use your precious energy

to build a magnificent life that really is

attainable. The miracle of your existence

calls for celebration every day. OPRAH WINFREY

Unlocking your potential.

Fighting the good fight.

Whatever my individual desires were to be free, I was not alone. There were many others who felt the same way.

ROSA PARKS

It takes courage for people

to listen to their own

goodness and act on it.

PABLO CASALS

A worthy cause.

Reaching out.

When you care,
people notice.

SUSANE BERGER

Each person represents

a world in us, a world

possibly not born until

they arrive, and it is only

by this meeting that a

new world is born. ANAIS NIN

Making a new friend.

An encouraging word.

Then something changed. One person came along and noticed my work and saw something in it. I'm not sure why, but she believed in me when others didn't. It's her faith in me that I celebrate today because that alone, at that particular time in my life, is what lit the fire that still burns today. WILLIAM ROGERS

Reminding one another of

the dream that each of us

aspires to may be enough

for us to set each other free.

ANTOINE DE SAINT-EXUPERY

Someone looking out for you.

Helping each other.

We must not, in trying to think about how we can make a big difference, ignore the small daily differences we can make which, over time, add up to the big differences that we often don't foresee.

MARIAN WRIGHT EDELMAN

Praise the bridge

that carried you over.

GEORGE COLMAN

A shoulder
to lean on.

The ocean is made of drops.   MOTHER TERESA

Working together.

A loyal friendship.

There are people who

take the heart out of you,

and there are people who

put it back. ELIZABETH DAVID

Leaving
a legacy.

We are here to add

what we can to,

not to get what we

can from, life.

SIR WILLIAM OSLER

We leave behind a bit

of ourselves wherever

we've been.

EDMOND HARACOURT

Giving
generously.

Getting involved.

What I do you cannot do; but what you do, I cannot do. The needs are great, and none of us, including me, ever do great things. But we can do small things, with great love, and together we can do something wonderful. MOTHER TERESA

Do your little bit of

good where you are;

it's those little bits of

good put together that

overwhelm the world.

DESMOND TUTU

Making a
difference.

Volunteering.

Sometimes you earn

more by doing things

that pay nothing.

TODD RUTHMAN

Sitting silently

beside a friend who

is hurting may be

the best gift we

can give. UNKNOWN

Being
necessary
to someone.

Smiles help me

remember that the

sky is only dark

between the stars.

NATHANIEL KENT LEATHAM

The kindness of strangers.

Feeling compassion.

When you begin to touch your heart or let your heart be touched, you begin to discover that it's bottomless, that it doesn't have any resolution, that this heart is huge, vast, and limitless. You begin to discover how much warmth and gentleness is there, as well as how much space. PEMA CHODRON

Being a good person.

The life I touch for good or ill will touch

another life, and that in turn another,

until who knows where the trembling stops

or in what far place my touch will be felt.

FREDERICK BUECHNER

Take the gentle path. GEORGE HERBERT

Living
harmlessly.

Within you there is a stillness and sanctuary to which you can retreat at anytime and be yourself. HERMANN HESSE

Being at peace.

Feeling
healthy.

Prevention is better than cure.   DESIDERIUS ERASMUS

Welcoming joy.

The moments of happiness take us by surprise. It is not that we seize them, but that they seize us. ASHLEY MONTAGU

Loosening up.

The world is your playground. Why aren't you playing? ELLIE KATZ

Having fun.

Pure and simple, any person who is enjoying life is a success.

WILLIAM FEATHER

Laughing
out loud.

Laughter is an

instant vacation.

MILTON BERLE

Unstructured play.

The less routine

the more life.

AMOS BRONSON ALCOTT

Being spontaneous.

Let the world slip we

shall ne'er be younger.

WILLIAM SHAKESPEARE

Enjoying the journey.

The best things in life are nearest: Breath in your nostrils, light in your eyes, flowers at your feet, duties at your hand, the path of right just before you. Then do not grasp at the stars, but do life's plain, common work as it comes, certain that daily duties and daily bread are the sweetest things in life. ROBERT LOUIS STEVENSON

What we call the secret of happiness is no more a secret than our willingness to choose life. LEO BUSCAGLIA

Being happy.

Taking
it all in.

...we get to think of life as an inexhaustible well. Yet everything happens once a certain number of times, and a very small number, really. How many more times will you remember a certain afternoon of your childhood, some afternoon that's so deeply a part of your being that you can't even conceive of your life without it? Perhaps four or five times more. Perhaps not even that. How many more times will you watch the full moon rise? Perhaps twenty. And yet it all seems so limitless. PAUL BOWLES

Do any human beings ever

realize life while they live it?

Every, every minute?

THORTON WILDER, OUR TOWN

Being there when you're there.

Taking the scenic route.

Improve your spare moments and they will become the brightest gems in your life.

RALPH WALDO EMERSON

We do not remember days,

we remember moments.

CESARE PAVESE

Creating memories.

Going where you've never been.

It doesn't matter what road you take, hill you climb, or path you're on, you will always end up in the same place, learning. RALPH STEVENSON

Nobody,

but nobody,

can make

it out

here alone.

MAYA ANGELOU

Shared strength.

The love of family and friends.

There are many compliments

that may come to an individual

in the course of a lifetime,

but there is no higher tribute

than to be loved by those who

know us best.   REV. DALE E. TURNER

What comes from

the heart goes to

the heart. UNKNOWN

An honest compliment.

Being grateful.

Treasure each other in the recognition that we

do not know how long we will have each other.

JOSHUA LIEBMAN

Lost, yesterday, somewhere between sunrise and sunset,

two golden hours, each set with sixty diamond minutes.

No reward is offered, for they are gone forever. HORACE MANN

Making
every
moment
count.

ISBN 1-932319-17-4

5 1 4 9 5

9 781932 319170

7 49190 02195 1